Interactive Vocabulary Lessons

Words to Know

Software Loading Instructions

To load the interactive whiteboard program onto your computer:

- Insert the CD into your computer.

- Once your computer recognizes the CD and you can see its contents on your monitor, drag the folder for the appropriate platform (PC or Mac) to your desktop.

  Note: You must drag the folder to your desktop and open the program from that folder to have all components work correctly. Opening from the CD may limit sounds and effects.

- Once the appropriate folder is open, double click the Flash file to open the program.

- Maximize the program to fill the entire monitor screen, go to your interactive device, and have fun teaching!

Software Registration

Please register your software to take advantage of software updates and special offers. Go to *http://www.ipinteractive.com/register* and simply complete the form. Thank you!

By Marjorie Frank and Jill Norris

Incentive Publications, Inc.
Nashville, Tennessee

Illustrated by Kathleen Bullock
Cover by Debbie Weekly
Copyedited by Cary Grayson

ISBN 978-0-86530-658-5

1   2   3   4   5   6   7   8   9   10   14   13   12   11

Printed by Sheridan Books, Inc., Chelsea, Michigan • April 2011
www.incentivepublications.com

Table of Contents

About This Program

Words to Know is a successful blend of high-tech and traditional classroom activities. The program includes a CD with a set of interactive digital whiteboard lessons to teach and practice vocabulary skills dealing with the robust vocabulary students should know and idioms and puns that can trip up English Language Learners. In addition, this teacher guide provides print support of the same skills.

Information is first introduced with an interactive *Learn It!* activity. These lessons include *Discuss It!* prompts. Following the introduction of words, students move through several interactive *Practice It!* lessons to help them plant those words firmly in their long-term memories. At the end of the unit, an interactive review activity encourages students to recall the words they have just learned.

The teacher guide includes:

- tips for each interactive screen;
- valuable printable resources that support the interactive whiteboard activities: glossary of terms used in this program, some common idioms, a few puns for fun, and tips for solving analogies;
- a cumulative review and assessment; and
- ten pages of paper-pencil practice encouraging students to use the new words they have learned.

Navigating the Whiteboard Activities

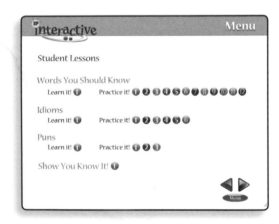

The Menu screen allows you to access any lesson or practice by touching its title.

Touch the Menu icon on any screen to move back to this screen.

Use the forward and back arrows  to move forward or backward one screen.

The reset icon allows you to clear work on a screen and restore it to its original look.

The numbers at the top of the screen indicate the number of *Learn It!* or *Practice It!* pages dealing with a specific skill. These numbers are active. Touch the number to move to that screen.

Print Support

Cumulative Review and Assessment

When the whole class, small groups, or individuals have completed the lessons, use the printable cumulative review and assessment to check students' understanding of the skills.

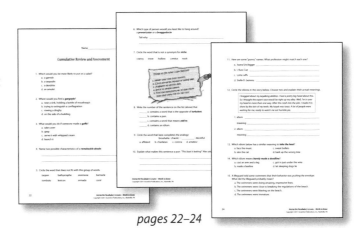

pages 22–24

Printable References

Imagine how handy it is to have a printable reference with a glossary of the terms used in this program, lists of idiom and puns, and a useful set of tips for solving analogies.

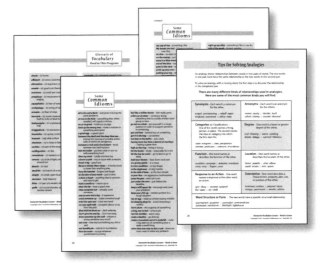

pages 25–28

Printable Practice Pages

Reinforce the skills taught in the interactive lessons with engaging paper-pencil practice activities. Each activity demands higher-level thinking and requires students to apply what they have learned.

pages 29–38

Vocabulary Standards and Skills Supported by This Program

Standard-Skill	Screens (Sc) • Pages (Pg)
Master the meaning of many new, grade-level appropriate vocabulary words; show understanding of word meaning	**Sc:** 4, 5, 6, 7, 8, 9, 10, 11, 12, 13, 14, 15, 16, 28 **Pg:** 29, 30, 31, 32, 33, 34
Use understanding of word meaning to make comparisons among words and meanings to choose the correct word or meaning for a specific situation	**Sc:** 4, 5, 6, 7, 8, 9, 10, 11, 12, 13, 14, 15, 28 **Pg:** 31, 33, 34
Use understanding of word meaning to make personal and real-life connections	**Sc:** 4, 5, 6, 7, 8, 9, 14, 15, 16 **Pg:** 31, 32
Use understanding of word meaning to set words into contexts such as place and purpose	**Sc:** 5, 6, 7, 8, 9, 10, 11, 12, 13, 14, 15, 16 **Pg:** 31, 32, 33, 34
Use understanding of new word meanings to solve various kinds of analogies	**Pg:** 33, 34
Give the meaning of common idioms; distinguish literal from actual meanings	**Sc:** 17, 18, 19, 20, 21, 22, 23 **Pg:** 35, 36
Compare meanings of idioms; choose the appropriate idiom for a context	**Sc:** 18, 19, 20, 21, 22 **Pg:** 35, 36
Recognize puns and understand the wordplay involved in a pun	**Sc:** 24, 25, 26, 27 **Pg:** 38
Identify the usage or vocabulary mix-up that contributes to a particular pun	**Sc:** 24, 26 **Pg:** 37, 38

Common Core Curriculum 6–12 Anchor Standards Supported by This Program

Anchor Standards for	Number and Category	Standard
Reading	**4:** Craft and Structure	Interpret words and phrases as they are used in a text, including determining technical, connotative, and figurative meanings, and analyze how specific word choices shape meaning or tone
Speaking and Listening	**2:** Comprehension and Collaboration	Integrate and evaluate information presented in diverse media and formats, including visually, quantitatively, and orally
Language	**4:** Vocabulary Acquisition and Use	Determine or clarify the meaning of unknown and multiple-meaning words and phrases by using context clues, analyzing meaningful word parts, and consulting general and specialized reference materials, as appropriate
Language	**5:** Vocabulary Acquisition and Use	Demonstrate understanding of word relationships and nuances in word meanings

Thinking Skills Supported by This Program
Structure Based on Bloom's Taxonomy of Cognitive Development

Cognitive Domain Levels Simplest ➝ Most Complex	Skills	Screens (Sc) and Pages (Pg)
Remembering: Recall data or information	arrange, define, describe, duplicate, label, list, match, name, order, recall, recognize, repeat, reproduce, select, state	**Sc:** 5, 6, 7, 8, 9, 10, 11, 12, 13, 14, 15, 16, 18, 19, 20, 21, 22, 23, 25, 26, 27, 28 **Pg:** 29, 30, 31, 32, 33, 34, 35, 36, 37, 38
Understanding: Understand the meaning, translation, interpolation, and interpretation of instructions and problems; explain concepts and state a problem in one's own words	classify, describe, discuss, explain, express, identify, indicate, locate, recognize, report, select, translate, paraphrase	**Sc:** 5, 6, 7, 8, 9, 10, 11, 12, 13, 14, 15, 16, 18, 19, 20, 21, 22, 23, 25, 26, 27, 28 **Pg:** 29, 30, 31, 32, 33, 34, 35, 36, 37, 38
Applying: Use a concept in a new situation or unprompted use of an abstraction	apply, choose, demonstrate, dramatize, employ, illustrate, interpret, operate, practice, schedule, sketch, solve, use, write	**Sc:** 4, 5, 6, 7, 8, 9, 10, 11, 12, 13, 14, 15, 16, 18, 19, 20, 21, 22, 23, 25, 26, 27, 28 **Pg:** 31, 32, 33, 34, 35, 36, 37, 38
Analyzing: Distinguish among component parts to arrive at meaning or understanding	analyze, appraise, calculate, categorize, compare, contrast, criticize, differentiate, discriminate, distinguish, examine, experiment, question, test	**Sc:** 4, 5, 6, 7, 8, 9, 10, 11, 12, 13, 14, 15, 18, 19, 20, 23, 25, 26, 27, 28 **Pg:** 30, 31, 32, 33, 34, 35, 36, 38
Evaluating: Justify a decision or position; make judgments about the value of an idea	appraise, argue, assess, defend, evaluate, judge, rate, select, support, value, compose, construct, create, design, develop, formulate, manage, organize, plan, prepare, propose, set up, write	**Sc:** 5, 6, 7, 8, 9, 10, 11, 12, 13, 14, 15, 18, 19, 20, 23, 25, 26, 27 **Pg:** 31, 32, 33, 34, 35, 36, 37, 38
Creating: Create a new product or viewpoint	assemble, construct, create, design, develop, formulate, mold, prepare, propose, synthesize, write	**Sc:** 5, 6, 7, 8, 9, 15 **Pg:** 32, 33, 34, 35, 38

Using Interactive Whiteboards in the Classroom

Interactive whiteboard activities help you capture student attention with content-rich, dynamic lessons, engaging your students in standards-based skill practice using hands-on activities that feel more like fun than work. Interactive whiteboards allow today's teachers to share ideas and information and to involve their students in learning with technology. Whiteboard activities offer shared learning experiences for large or small groups, as well as high-interest practice for individuals.

One-computer classrooms can maximize the use of limited computer access by using the whiteboard. Students work together with individuals contributing at the board, other participants at the computer, and the group as a whole discussing the activity. The participation that transpires between the person at the computer, the users at the board, and the computer itself is a unique and very adaptable arrangement.

Whiteboard activities accommodate different learning styles. Tactile learners benefit from touching and marking at the board, audio learners listen to audio prompts and class discussions, while visual learners can see what is taking place as it develops at the board.

Interactive whiteboards can be a helpful tool for differentiating learning. Learners have a large focal point and a colorful image that focuses their attention. The whiteboard motivates reluctant learners, but it also appeals to both higher- and lower-level learners.

Teachers easily integrate digital whiteboard instruction to meet standards requiring teaching with technology.

Tips for Getting Started

1) Choose the location of your interactive board carefully. Consider whether large windows will require blinds on a sunny day. Think about the height of viewers. Remember that a board and extra equipment can require as many as six nearby electric sockets.

2) If something doesn't work, don't be afraid to ask a student for help.

3) Take any training classes that are offered to you. Then adapt the recommendations to fit your classroom.

4) Don't limit interactive whiteboard use to whole-group presentations. It is a valuable tool for small-group instruction and individual practice.

5) Be sensitive to the middle-school student's fear of looking different and being wrong. Some students may prefer to work in teams.

6) Using digital video cameras, voting systems, and scanners with your whiteboard can take your lessons to very exciting places. Document cameras are extremely powerful when used with an interactive whiteboard. They project onto the board anything placed under them.

7) Record your instruction and post the material for review by students at a later time.

Screen-by-Screen Teacher Tips

Words You Should Know

Learn It!   1 (page 10)

Practice It!

1 (page 10)	2 (page 11)	3 (page 11)
4 (page 12)	5 (page 12)	6 (page 13)
7 (page 13)	8 (page 14)	9 (page 14)
10 (page 15)	11 (page 15)	12 (page 15)

Idioms

Learn It!   1 (page 16)

Practice It!

1 (page 16)	2 (page 17)	3 (page 17)	4 (page 17)
5 (page 18)	6 (page 18)		

Puns

Learn It!   1 (page 19)

Practice It!

1 (page 19)	2 (page 20)	3 (page 20)

Show You Know It!

1 (page 21)

Screen-by-Screen Teacher Tips

Words to Know **Learn It! 1**

As you introduce this lesson, remind students of the ways they might discover the meanings of words new to them:

- Using the structure of words—prefixes, suffixes, and roots—to determine the word's meaning

- Paying attention to the context around a word and considering its denotation and connotation

- Learning pairs of confusing words

It is also important that students are successfully able to navigate a glossary or a dictionary. Touch the screen to reveal a talk bubble with an example (*tangle*). Point out the dictionary entry for *tangle* and discuss the best definition for the way the word is used in the cartoon.

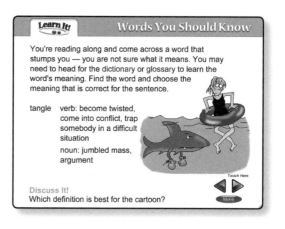

Words to Know **Practice It! 1**

Reproduce the printable glossary provided on page 25 or provide dictionaries for students to use as they complete the next lesson. Invite students to check the meaning of any unknown words and then to answer the questions. Have them justify their responses by telling why or why not. Then touch the *yes* or *no* to confirm the correct answer. Occasionally students will logically justify a "wrong" answer; if the justification makes sense, accept the answer.

1. no
2. yes
3. yes
4. no
5. no

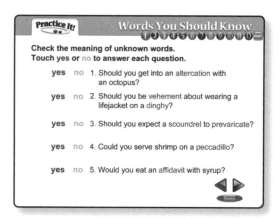

Words to Know   Practice It! 2

Reproduce the printable glossary provided on page 25 or provide dictionaries for students to use as they complete the next lesson. Invite students to check the meaning of any unknown words and then to answer the questions. Have them justify their responses by telling why or why not. Then touch the *yes* or *no* to confirm the correct answer. Occasionally students will logically justify a "wrong" answer; if the justification makes sense, accept the answer.

1. yes
2. yes
3. no
4. yes
5. no

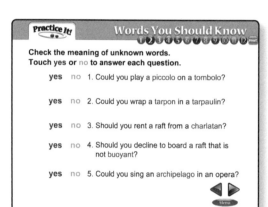

Words to Know   Practice It! 3

Continue the activity from the previous screens.

1. no
2. no
3. yes
4. no
5. no

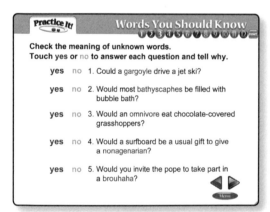

Words to Know Practice It! 4

Challenge students to read the three bits of good advice and to explain why the advice is good. Their explanations will require some knowledge about the meanings of the words in the sentence. The definition of each blue word appears when the correct photo is touched.

> Some jellyfish have a paralyzing sting, so it's a good idea to keep your snout (nose) away from them.

> Waterskiing behind a sleeping boat driver is a dangerous idea.

> Anemones are pokey, spiked creatures. They are not good "handshakers."

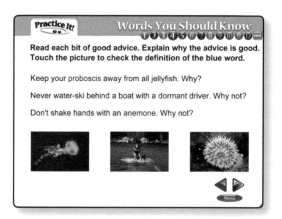

Words to Know Practice It! 5

Continue the activity from the previous screen with three more bits of good advice.

> A lifeguard who is afraid of water isn't a reliable rescuer.

> Seaweed can wrap around you as you swim, so it's best to swim where there isn't any.

> No one wants an incompetent dive instructor!

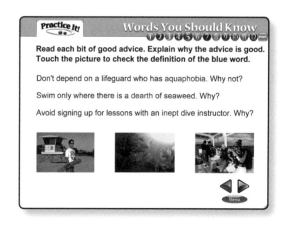

Words to Know   Practice It! 6

Have dictionaries or the printable glossary on page 25 available for student use. Challenge students to look up the meaning of each blue word and then evaluate the four phrases below the word and choose one that is a place where you would find it. Touch the phrase to check the answer.

armada—in the ocean

garnish—on a baked fish

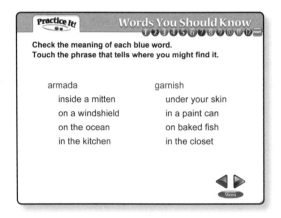

Words to Know   Practice It! 7

Continue the activity from the previous screen.

tourniquet—around a leg

corona—around the sun

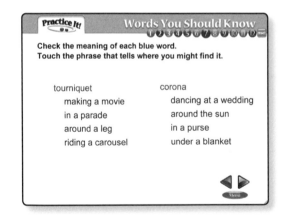

Words to Know   Practice It! 8

Have dictionaries or the printable glossary on page 25 available for student use. Challenge students to look up the meaning of each blue word and then evaluate the four phrases below the word and choose one that is a place where you would find it. Touch the phrase to check the answer.

pinnacle—on a cathedral

lexicon—in a library

Words to Know   Practice It! 9

Continue the activity from the previous screen.

dendrite—in a nerve cell

cochlea—in your ear

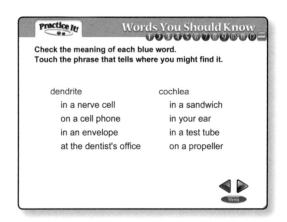

Words to Know Practice It! 10

Read this list of words aloud for students. Enjoy the sounds of these seven nouns. Challenge students to use the glossary or dictionary to look up any unknown words and determine which one could be found in the bag.

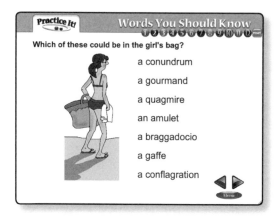

Words to Know Practice It! 11

On this screen students will check the meanings of unfamiliar nouns and select the phrase that describes what to do with the thing. Check the selected phrase to check the answer.

After successfully completing the screen, challenge students to choose a new word and compose a similar problem.

     a neophyte—teach it

     an antiphony—sing it

     a mandrake—plant it

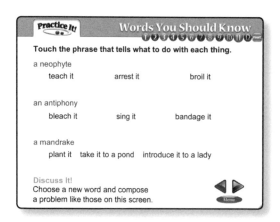

Words to Know Practice It! 12

Invite students to match the animals with their homes. When the correct phrase is dragged into the box by the animal's name, a photo of the home will appear.

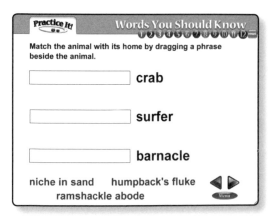

Idioms   Learn It! 1

Introduce or review the term *idiom*. Explain that an idiom is one kind of figurative language and that figurative language is a way of using language that expands the (actual) meaning of the words and gives them a new or more interesting twist.

Discuss the examples, having students explain each idiom's meaning versus the actual meaning of the words. Touch the octopus to see and hear another idiom.

A printable list of idioms is available on pages 26 and 27.

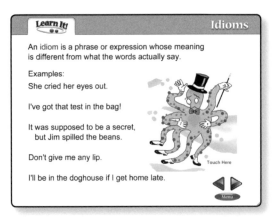

Idioms   Practice It! 1

This screen requires students to identify idioms in the talk bubble and match them to meanings given on the screen. Ultimately, they are trying to determine which meaning in the list doesn't represent one of the idioms in the cartoon.

> in deep trouble

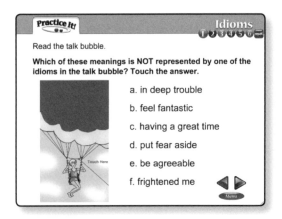

Idioms   Practice It! 2

Challenge students to find the idiom in each problem that has a meaning most similar to the blue idiom. Touch the selected idiom to check the answer.

1. Now you're between a rock and a hard place.

2. Snorkeling is my cup of tea.

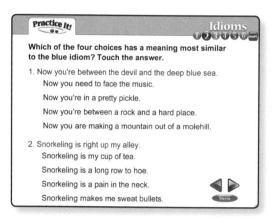

Which of the four choices has a meaning most similar to the blue idiom? Touch the answer.

1. Now you're between the devil and the deep blue sea.
   Now you need to face the music.
   Now you're in a pretty pickle.
   Now you're between a rock and a hard place.
   Now you are making a mountain out of a molehill.

2. Snorkeling is right up my alley.
   Snorkeling is my cup of tea.
   Snorkeling is a long row to hoe.
   Snorkeling is a pain in the neck.
   Snorkeling makes me sweat bullets.

Idioms   Practice It! 3

The paragraph at the top of the screen gives important background to the reader. Read it together and then challenge students to identify idioms that would not be useful when Damon speaks to his friends.

Neither *You are barking up the wrong tree by asking me* nor *It'll be a red-letter day when I do this* communicate the idea that Damon wants to get across.

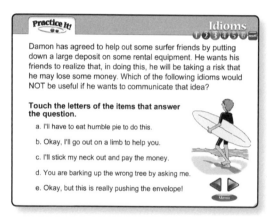

Damon has agreed to help out some surfer friends by putting down a large deposit on some rental equipment. He wants his friends to realize that, in doing this, he will be taking a risk that he may lose some money. Which of the following idioms would NOT be useful if he wants to communicate that idea?

Touch the letters of the items that answer the question.

a. I'll have to eat humble pie to do this.

b. Okay, I'll go out on a limb to help you.

c. I'll stick my neck out and pay the money.

d. You are barking up the wrong tree by asking me.

e. Okay, but this is really pushing the envelope!

Idioms   Practice It! 4

Challenge students to choose an idiom to match each definition. Touch the selected idiom to check your choice.

just right—on the money

in great shape—mint condition

slow down and wait—hold your horses

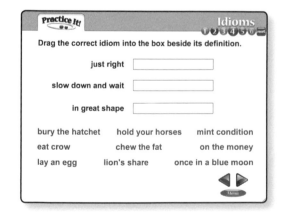

Drag the correct idiom into the box beside its definition.

just right	
slow down and wait	
in great shape	

bury the hatchet   hold your horses   mint condition

eat crow   chew the fat   on the money

lay an egg   lion's share   once in a blue moon

Idioms   Practice It! 5

Two idioms in each set have similar meanings and one does not. Challenge students to use what they know about the meanings of the idioms to identify the misfit.

1. an ace in the whole

2. make a beeline

3. died with his boots on

4. rake over the coals

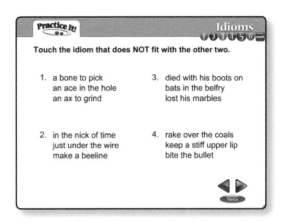

Idioms   Practice It! 6

Each of these photos suggests the actual meaning of the words in a common idiom. Challenge students to identify each idiom. Touch the photo to make the words appear. Then invite students to drag the meaning of the idiom under the words.

barking up the wrong tree—making a false assumption

put foot in the mouth—say something stupid

holds a candle to—measures up to

in the doghouse—in big trouble

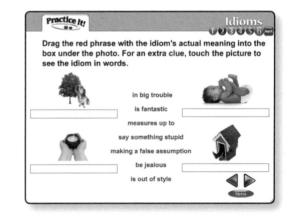

Puns   Learn It! 1

Introduce or review the meaning of a pun—*a phrase that makes a play on words*. Read the examples together and challenge students to explain the play on words in each one.

> crew cut: reduction in staff, or style of haircut
>
> pool: to combine resources, or a large artificial basin filled with water for swimming
>
> pain: unpleasant physical sensation, or somebody troublesome
>
> dough: mixture of flour and water, or money

For a printable list of examples, see page 27.

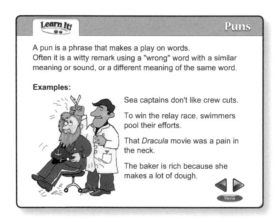

A pun is a phrase that makes a play on words. Often it is a witty remark using a "wrong" word with a similar meaning or sound, or a different meaning of the same word.

Examples:

Sea captains don't like crew cuts.

To win the relay race, swimmers pool their efforts.

That *Dracula* movie was a pain in the neck.

The baker is rich because she makes a lot of dough.

Puns   Practice It! 1

As your students read the puns on this page, invite them to explain the play on words. Once they have identified the nonpun (f.), challenge them to think of a way to change the optometrist's name so that the sentence is a pun. (*Dr. I. Tester* or *Dr. C. A. Biggee* are two possibilities).

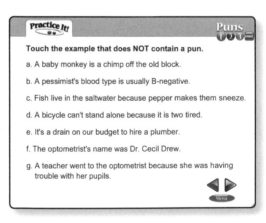

Touch the example that does NOT contain a pun.

a. A baby monkey is a chimp off the old block.

b. A pessimist's blood type is usually B-negative.

c. Fish live in the saltwater because pepper makes them sneeze.

d. A bicycle can't stand alone because it is two tired.

e. It's a drain on our budget to hire a plumber.

f. The optometrist's name was Dr. Cecil Drew.

g. A teacher went to the optometrist because she was having trouble with her pupils.

Puns   Practice It! 2

Invite students to distinguish between two common categories of puns: puns that use a wrong homophone in place of the right one or puns that play on different meanings of the same word. Drag a starfish into the correct column to mark the answers.

Different Meanings—1, 2, and 3

Wrong Homophone—4

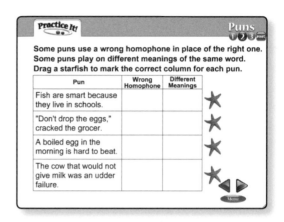

Puns   Practice It! 3

Challenge students to read the names on the lockers and choose the job that each person does. When the job is dragged into the box on the correct locker, it will remain in place.

Burnett N. Peele	sunbather
Wanna Ketchum	fisherwoman
Claude Daly	crab catcher
Russ Cue	lifeguard
Seymour Squidd	snorkeler

Show You Know It! 1

Read the statement at the top of the screen. Have a student touch the portion of the grid with the correct meaning. The rectangle will flip to a new statement. Continue touching the meanings until the nine parts of the grid have flipped to reveal a photograph of fun on the beach.

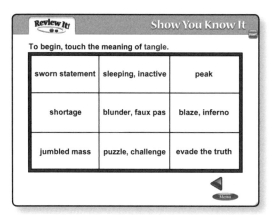

sworn statement	sleeping, inactive	peak
shortage	blunder, faux pas	blaze, inferno
jumbled mass	puzzle, challenge	evade the truth

To begin, touch the meaning of *tangle*.

To begin, touch the meaning of *tangle*.   (jumbled mass)

Touch the meaning of *affidavit*.   (sworn statement)

Touch the meaning of *prevaricate*.   (evade the truth)

Touch the meaning of *dormant*.   (sleeping, inactive)

Touch the meaning of *dearth*.   (shortage)

Touch the meaning of *pinnacle*.   (peak)

Touch the meaning of *conundrum*.   (puzzle, challenge)

Touch the meaning of *gaffe*.   (blunder, faux pas)

Touch the meaning of *conflagration*.   (blaze, inferno)

Cumulative Review and Assessment

1. Which would you be most likely to put on a salad?
    a. a garnish
    b. a tarpaulin
    c. a dendrite
    d. an amulet

2. Where would you find a **gargoyle**?
    a. near a sink, holding a bottle of mouthwash
    b. trying to extinguish a conflagration
    c. rowing a dinghy
    d. on the side of a building

3. What would you do if someone made a **gaffe**?
    a. take cover
    b. gasp
    c. serve it with whipped cream
    d. launch it

4. Name two possible characteristics of a **ramshackle abode**:

    _____

    _____

5. Circle the word that does not fit with this group of words.

    tarpon   bathyscaphe   anemone   barnacle

    tombolo   lexicon   armada   coral

6. Which type of person would you least like to hang around?
   a **prevaricator** or a **braggadocio**

   Tell why: _____

   _____

7. Circle the word that is not a synonym for **niche**.

   cranny   trove   hollow   crevice   nook

Things to Do After I Get Rescued

1. Never wear the color maroon.
2. Climb pinnacles instead of sailing seas.
3. Augment my all-fish diet.
4. Stick to serene waters.
5. Find the manufacturer of that faulty boat and chew him (or her) out!

8. Write the number of the sentence on the list (above) that

   _____ a. contains a word that is the opposite of **turbulent**.

   _____ b. contains a pun.

   _____ c. contains a word that means **add to**.

   _____ d. contains an idiom.

9. Circle the word that best completes the analogy:
                 brouhaha : chaotic : : _____ : deceitful
   a. affidavit   b. charlatan   c. corona   d. amateur

10. Explain what makes this sentence a pun: *"This boat is leaking!" Alex said balefully.*

    _____

    _____

    _____

11. Here are some "punny" names. What profession might match each one?

    a. Juana Unclogger _____

    b. I. Russ Cue _____

    c. Lotta Laffs _____

    d. Stella D. Gemms _____

12. Circle the idioms in the story below. Choose two and explain their actual meanings.

> *I bragged about my kayaking abilities. I had a pretty big head about this. So I thought the expert race would be right up my alley. Well, I'm in over my head in more than one way. After the crash into the pier, I made it to shore by the skin of my teeth. My kayak was toast. A lot of people were waiting for me, ready to watch me eat humble pie.*

    1. idiom _____

       meaning _____

    2. idiom _____

       meaning _____

13. Which idiom below has a similar meaning to **take the heat**?

    a. face the music   c. sweat bullets

    b. skin the cat   d. bark up the wrong tree

14. Which idiom means **barely made a deadline**?

    a. cost an arm and a leg   c. got in just under the wire

    b. made a beeline   d. let sleeping dogs lie

15. A lifeguard told some swimmers that their behavior was *pushing the envelope*. What did the lifeguard probably mean?

    a. The swimmers were doing amazing, impressive feats.

    b. The swimmers were close to breaking the regulations of the beach.

    c. The swimmers were littering on the beach.

    d. The swimmers were immature.

abode – (n) home

affidavit – (n) sworn statement

altercation – (n) argument or fight

amulet – (n) good luck charm

anemone – (n) small sea creature

antiphony – (n) responsive chanting or singing

aquaphobia – (n) fear of water

archipelago – (n) string of islands

armada – (n) fleet of ships

barnacle – (n) ocean creature that attaches itself to rocks or boat hulls

bathyscaphe – (n) a submersible exploration ship

braggadocio – (n) someone who brags a lot

brouhaha – (n) uproar, confusion

buoyant – (adj) able to float

charlatan – (n) a cheat or faker

cochlea – (n) part of the inner ear

conflagration – (n) fire

conundrum – (n) mystery or puzzle

corona – (n) circle of light; ring of light around sun

dearth – (n) lack

dendrite – (n) branch of a nerve cell

dinghy – (n) small, open boat or rubber raft

dormant – (adj) sleeping

fluke – (n) part of a whale's tail

gaffe – (n) a social blunder, especially a tactless remark

gargoyle – (n) grotesque carved stone feature with a spout designed to carry rainwater away from a building

garnish – (n) decoration (often on food)

gourmand – (n) big eater

inept – (adj) clumsy

lexicon – (n) dictionary

mandrake – (n) a plant of the nightshade family

neophyte – (n) a beginner

niche – (n) corner or cubbyhole

nonagenarian – (n) person aged 90–99

omnivore – (n) one who eats all kinds of food

peccadillo – (n) a minor sin

piccolo – (n) small flute–like musical instrument

pinnacle – (n) the highest point

proboscis – (n) nose

quagmire – (n) sticky situation

ramshackle – (adj) run-down

scoundrel – (n) crook

tangle – (v) become twisted; trap someone; get into conflict; (n) jumbled mass; argument

tarpon – (n) a large, silvery fish of the Atlantic coastal waters

tarpaulin – (n) canvas cover

tombolo – sand or gravel deposit that connects an island to the mainland

tourniquet – (n) compression bandage used to temporarily stop blood flow

vehement – (adj) enthusiastic

Some Common Idioms

all in the same boat – everyone is facing the same problems

an ace in the hole – something that, when revealed, will supply a victory

an ax to grind – holding a grudge

bark up the wrong tree – make a mistake in something attempted

a good egg – a good sport

between the devil and the deep blue sea – having two courses of possible action, both of which are dangerous

between a rock and a hard place – stuck between two hard options

bite the bullet – put fear aside or put up with something hard

blew my mind – totally shocked me

a bone to pick – has an issue with someone

break a leg – good luck

Blood is thicker than water. – A family bond is closer than anything else.

bury the hatchet – forgive and forget

by the skin of your teeth – just in time

a dime a dozen – anything that is common and easy to get

hold a candle to – match up to

chew the fat – have a good chat

chew someone out – verbally scold someone

cost an arm and a leg – is expensive

crack someone up – make someone laugh

cried her eyes out – cried very hard

cry over spilt milk – complain about a loss from the past

died with his boots on – died violently

Don't give me any lip. – Don't be sassy.

drive someone up the wall – irritate or annoy someone very much

eat crow – take back something you did or said

eat humble pie – submit to humiliation

face the music – accept whatever punishment is coming

feel like a million bucks – feel really great

a fish out of water – someone doing something that is outside of their usual group or area

go out on a limb – put yourself in a tough position in order to support someone or something

got cold feet – backed out of something

got it in the bag – succeeded

has bats in the belfry – acts crazy

having more fun than a barrel of monkeys – having a great time

high on the hog – living in luxury

hit the books – study—especially for a test

hit the hay (or sack) – go to bed or go to sleep

hold your horses – slow down and wait

in a pretty pickle – in a mess

in mint condition – in top shape

in the doghouse – in big trouble

in the nick of time – at the last minute

in your face – an aggressive confrontation

jump the gun – start too soon

just under the wire – just before the deadline

keep a stiff upper lip – be tough and cover your emotions

keep your chin up – remain positive in a tough situation

lay an egg – make an embarrassing mistake

let sleeping dogs lie – avoid restarting a conflict

lion's share – the majority of something

a long row to hoe – a hard job

lost his marbles – went crazy

make a beeline – go directly

make a mountain out of a molehill – make a big deal out of something that is really a small thing

more than one way to skin a cat – there are many ways to solve any problem

(continued)

Some Common Idioms

my cup of tea – something I like

My hands are tied. – I have no control over this.

no dice – to reject an idea or disagree

on the money – just right

once in a blue moon – rarely

out of the blue – sudden and unexpected

pain in the neck – annoying person

prick up your ears – listen very carefully

pulling your leg – playing a joke on someone

pushing the envelope – pushing boundaries, rules, or possibilities

put your foot in your mouth – say something stupid or embarrassing

rake over the coals – scold or berate someone

a red-letter day – a great day

right up my alley – something I like or can do

salt of the earth – honest, reliable

skating on thin ice – doing something risky

smell a rat – detect that someone in a group is betraying the others

smell something fishy – sensing that something isn't right

spilled the beans – told something that was supposed to be secret

steal someone's thunder – take credit for something that someone else did

stick out your neck – take a chance

sweating bullets – very nervous

take the bull by the horns – take strong action; make something happen

went over like a lead balloon – was poorly received by another or an audience

whole nine yards – all of it, everything

A Few Puns for Fun

I used to have a fear of hurdles, but I got over it.

Her desire to be a dermatologist was only skin deep.

The dentist and the manicurist fought tooth and nail.

My surgeon is so funny—she keeps me in stitches.

A clockmaker works overtime.

A pessimist's blood type is always B-negative.

Custer wore Arrow shirts.

Nacho cheese is cheese that is not yours.

It was a drain on our budget to hire a plumber.

Is a barber who works in a library called a barbarian?

I heard that the origami store down the street just folded.

The guy who invented the door knocker got a No-Bell Prize.

Everybody cried at the wedding. Even the cake was in tiers.

Students were delighted when the electricity went off during a storm.

Skipping school to go bungee jumping will get you suspended.

Sue says she dreams in color. I say that's a pigment of her imagination.

When I saw that the surgeon's name was Dr. Slaughter, I cancelled the appointment.

Tips for Solving Analogies

An analogy shows relationships between words in two pairs of words. The two words in one pair must have the same relationship as the two words in the second pair.

To solve an analogy with a missing word, the first step is to discover the relationship in the completed pair.

There are many different kinds of relationships used in analogies. Here are some of the most common kinds you will find.

Synonyms – Each word is a synonym for the other.

insipid : uninteresting :: rebuff : reject
vindicate : exonerate :: abhor : hate

Antonyms – Each word is an antonym for the others.

mania : sanity :: slander : truth
adroit : clumsy :: ascend : descend

Categories (or Classification) – One of the words names a thing, person, or place. The second names the class or category into which the first item fits.

cedar : evergreen :: sleet : precipitation
attorney : profession :: anemone : invertebrate

Degree – One word is a lesser or greater degree of the other.

cool : freezing :: warm : scalding
drizzle : deluge :: comical : hilarious

Function – One word names or describes the function of the other.

candidate : campaign :: detective : investigate
whisk : whip :: flippers : swim

Location – One word names or describes the location of the other.

femur : patella :: ulna : elbow
squid : ocean :: aria : opera

Response to an Action – One word names a response to the other word, an action.

spin : dizzy :: overeat : satiated
fire : sears :: ice : chills

Descriptive – One word describes a characteristic, property, part, use, or position of the other.

luminous : embers :: piquant : tacos
hungry : gourmand :: nimble : athlete

Word Structure or Form – The two words have a specific structural relationship.

postmortem : posterior :: contradict : contraindicate
quicksand : sandstorm :: flashlight : lighthouse

Underwater Jumble

The legendary sea monster, the Kraken, was known for its gargantuan size and long tentacles. Some say that the Kraken was a great gourmand. Write a word to match each clue definition, putting one letter on each space. Then, follow the directions below to answer a question about the Kraken.

1. **confusion**
   ___ ⬡ a ___ ⬡

2. **generosity**
   ___ ⬡ ___ g ___ ⬡ ⬡

3. **draw conclusions based on evidence**
   ⬡ ___ ⬡ ___ r ___

4. **act of a hero**
   ⬡ e ___ ___ ⬡ ___ ___

5. **heavy and laborious**
   ⬡ ___ ⬡ ⬡ e ___ ___ ___ ___

Write the letters from the circles.

Unscramble the letters to answer the question:

WHAT DID THE KRAKEN EAT?

Answer:

___ ___ ___ ___   ___ ___ ___

___ ___ ___ ___ ___

Interactive Vocabulary Lessons—Words to Know

Practice with New Words

WORDS IN HIDING

Each of the words shown is hiding within a longer word.
Follow the definition clues to complete each of the bigger words.

1. __ __ __ __ __ __ c a p __ __
   (SUBMERSIBLE EXPLORATION SHIP)

2. __ __ __ f l a g __ __ __ __ __ __
   (A LARGE, DESTRUCTIVE FIRE)

3. __ __ __ s h a c k __ __
   (RUNDOWN)

4. __ __ u r n __ __ __ __ __
   (COMPRESSION BANDAGE USED TO STOP BLEEDING)

5. __ m u l e __
   (GOOD LUCK CHARM)

6. __ e a r __ __
   (LACK)

7. __ __ c h i p __ __ __ __ __
   (STRING OF ISLANDS)

8. __ __ __ __ h a h a
   (UPROAR OR CONFUSION)

Name _____

Would You? Could You? Should You?

To answer the questions well, you'll need to know (or find) the meanings of the bold words. Answer each question yes or no. Then give a brief reason for your answer.

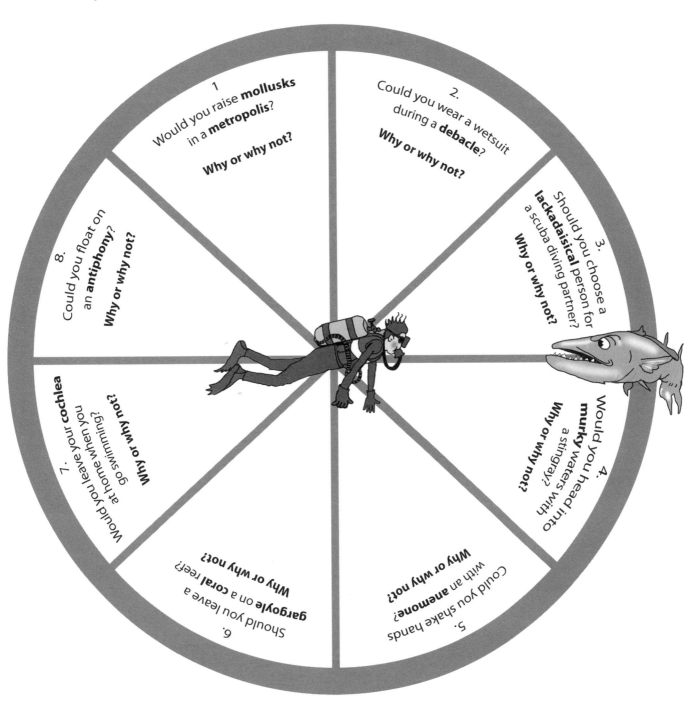

1. Would you raise **mollusks** in a **metropolis**?

   Why or why not?

2. Could you wear a wetsuit during a **debacle**?

   Why or why not?

3. Should you choose a **lackadaisical** person for a scuba diving partner?

   Why or why not?

4. Would you head into **murky** waters with a stingray?

   Why or why not?

5. Could you shake hands with an **anemone**?

   Why or why not?

6. Should you leave a **gargoyle** on a coral reef?

   Why or why not?

7. Would you leave your **cochlea** at home when you go swimming?

   Why or why not?

8. Could you float on an **antiphony**?

   Why or why not?

Double the Fun

Show that you know the meaning of the bold word by following the directions **to name two . . .**

A. WAYS FOR SOMEONE WITH **AQUAPHOBIA** TO HAVE FUN AT THE BEACH:

1.

2.

B. PLACES YOU MIGHT FIND A **BARNACLE**:

1.

2.

C. THINGS A **DORMANT** SAILOR MIGHT DO:

1.

2.

D. REASONS TO AVOID AN **ALTERCATION** WITH A BARRACUDA:

1.

2.

E. MANEUVERS AN **INEPT** SURFER SHOULD NOT ATTEMPT:

1.

2.

F. PLACES TO TIE UP A **DINGHY**:

1.

2.

G. THINGS THAT ARE PROBABLY NOT **BUOYANT**:

1.

2.

H. CHARACTERISTICS OF A SWORDFISH'S **PROBOSCIS**:

1.

2.

Name _____

Interactive Vocabulary Lessons—Words to Know
Copyright ©2011 INCENTIVE PUBLICATIONS, Inc., Nashville, TN

Analogy Challenge

Choose one word from the box below to complete each analogy.

	WORD 1	IS TO	WORD 2	AS	WORD 3	IS TO	WORD 4
1	dinghy	:	surface	::	bathyscaphe	:	
2	mud	:	quagmire	::		:	pinnacle
3	piquant	:		::	surreptitious	:	thief
4	adept	:	inept	::		:	dishonest
5	dissect	:		::	thermal	:	thermometer
6		:	minor	::	enraged	:	piqued

nadir pinpoint barnacle diver debris egregious sneaky fraud
adapt peeked candid disturb query enchilada zenith
undersea deceitful section quandary quarrel

Name _____

Repeat Relationships

To solve an analogy, start by evaluating the relationship between the pair of words you are given. Then apply that same relationship to the other pair. Decide the relationship for each analogy. Write the code letter at the beginning. Then circle the word that best completes the analogy.

_____ 1. channel : buoy : : _____ : aria
   a. opera   c. aorta
   b. airport   d. ocean

_____ 2. observant : lifeguard : : articulate : _____
   a. loquacious   c. attorney
   b. argumentative   d. architecture

_____ 3. _____ : vacillate : : repose : rest
   a. roam   c. vacate
   b. waiver   d. relax

_____ 4. snorkel : _____ : : flippers : swim
   a. head   c. mask
   b. oxygen   d. breathe

_____ 5. tired : exhausted : : _____ : bully
   a. rested   c. tease
   b. berate   d. rascal

_____ 6. shrimp : _____ : : diamond : mineral
   a. ocean   c. lobster
   b. restaurant   d. crustacean

_____ 7. disapprove : condone : : _____ : pretentious
   a. concur   c. arrogant
   b. deceptive   d. humble

_____ 8. submersible : substandard : : _____ : retrofit
   a. submarine   c. retrograde
   b. retool   d. supercede

CODES

S = synonyms
A = antonyms
C = same category
D = degree
DS = descriptive
F = function
L = location
W = word form
R = response or action

Name _____

Interactive Vocabulary Lessons—Words to Know
Copyright ©2011 Incentive Publications, Inc., Nashville, TN

They Don't Mean What They Say

Each picture shows the literal meaning of an English-language idiom.
Write the idiom beneath the picture. Tell its actual meaning.

The idiom:

What it means:

The idiom:

What it means:

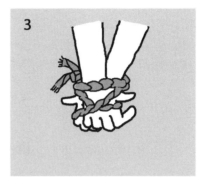

The idiom:

What it means:

The idiom:

What it means:

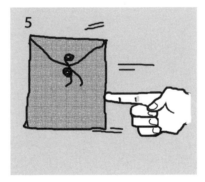

The idiom:

What it means:

The idiom:

What it means:

Draw the literal meaning of any idiom
that you choose.

Write the idiom:

Write its meaning:

Name _____

Interactive Vocabulary Lessons—Words to Know

Which Idiom?

Circle the idiom or idioms that best answer the question.

1 Which idiom has a meaning similar to that of *have a bone to pick*?

- A. JUMP THE GUN
- B. LET SLEEPING DOGS LIE
- C. MAKE A BEELINE
- D. HAVE AN AXE TO GRIND

2 Rozzie has just mastered a skating move. Which idiom fits?

- A. SHE'S GOT BATS IN THE BELFRY.
- B. SHE'S IN A PRETTY PICKLE.
- C. SHE'S SKATING ON THIN ICE.
- D. SHE'S GOT IT IN THE BAG.

3 Which idiom has a meaning opposite to the meaning of *butter up*?

- A. CHEW SOMEONE OUT
- B. PULL YOUR LEG
- C. CRY OVER SPILT MILK
- D. SKATE ON THIN ICE

4 You *smell something fishy* about the way someone is treating a friend. Which idioms give good advice for what you might do?

- A. TAKE THE BULL BY THE HORNS
- B. HIT THE HAY
- C. GO OUT ON A LIMB
- D. STICK OUT YOUR NECK

5 If someone is a *pain in the neck*, which idiom(s) describe other characteristics this person might have?

- A. HE'S (SHE'S) THE SALT OF THE EARTH.
- B. HE'S (SHE'S) YOUR CUP OF TEA.
- C. HE (SHE) DRIVES YOU UP THE WALL.
- D. HE'S (SHE'S) IN YOUR FACE.

6 Which idiom has a meaning opposite to the meaning of *carry a chip on your shoulder*?

- A. BURY THE HATCHET
- B. JUST UNDER THE WIRE
- C. LIVE HIGH ON THE HOG
- D. SPILL THE BEANS

7 Which idiom gives good advice of what to do after you *stick your foot in your mouth*?

- A. EAT CROW
- B. EAT HUMBLE PIE
- C. BE A GOOD EGG
- D. NONE OF THE ABOVE
- E. ALL OF THE ABOVE

WE'RE ALL IN THE SAME BOAT NOW!

Name _____

WHOSE LOCKER?

The lockers at the gym are labeled with the professions of gym members. Let the names help you decide whose locker is whose! Write the name of the locker owner on each locker.

105 Comedian

106 Engineer

107 Physical Therapist

108 Librarian

109 Nutritionist

115 Optician

116 Chef

117 Attorney

118 Magician

119 Reservationist

LOCKER OWNERS

Justin Credabul
Bill D. Bridges
Chris P. Bacon
Leigh Vatipp

Eaton Wright
Cy Lance
Ken U. Seamy
Ben Jerelbo

Hugh Morrus
Caldwell A. Head
Sue Yiu
Buck Ineer

There are two extra names on the list. Think of an appropriate profession for each of them. Write it below the name.

Name _____

The Fun in the Pun

Think about what's behind the fun in a pun. For each pun, give a brief explanation of what the "word trick" is that makes the pun. Use the lines at the bottom, or write on the back of the paper.

1.
Favorite lullaby of fishermen and fisherwomen: "Now I Filet Me Down to Sleep"

2.
A mosquito's favorite sport is skin-diving.

3.
The octopus was well armed when he got into an altercation with the squid.

4.
To win a relay race, swimmers pool their efforts.

5.
Want to communicate with a fish? Drop him a line.

6.
Least favorite song of surfers: "Shark! The Herald Angels Sing!"

7.
The only way to stop a charging killer whale is to take away his credit card.

8.
Someone told me I was indecisive. I'm not sure if it's true.

9.
When 5000 hares escaped the zoo, police combed the area.

10.
If you read books while you sunbathe, you'll be well red.

11. Create your own pun!

1. _____

2. _____

3. _____

4. _____

5. _____

6. _____

7. _____

8. _____

9. _____

10. _____

Name _____

Answer Key

Cumulative Review and Assessment, pages 22–24

1. a
2. d
3. b
4. Answers will vary. Check to see that student answers show understanding of the meanings of ramshackle and abode.
5. lexicon
6. Answers will vary. Check to see that student adequately explains his or her choice.
7. trove
8. a. 4 (serene)
   b. 1 (maroon)
   c. 3 (augment)
   d. 5 (chew him or her out)
9. b
10. The adverb "balefully" plays against the idea of a leaking boat.
11. Answers will vary:
    Possible answers:
    a. plumber
    b. lifeguard, rescue worker, firefighter
    c. comedienne
    d. thief
12. The story has six idioms that should
    be circled:
    • had a pretty big head
    • right up my alley
    • in over my head
    • by the skin of my teeth
    • kayak was toast
    • eat humble pie

Student explanations of meanings will vary. Check to see that they have the right idea of the idiom meaning.

13. a
14. c
15. b

Paper and Pencil Practice, pages 29–38

p. 29
1. chaos
2. largess
3. infer
4. heroism
5. ponderous
Answer: fish and ships

p. 30
1. bathyscaphe
2. conflagration
3. ramshackle
4. tourniquet
5. amulet
6. dearth
7. archipelago
8. brouhaha

p. 31
Answers will vary. Check to see that student gives a reasonable explanation for his or her answer to each question.

p. 32
Answers will vary. Check to see that student gives a reasonable explanation for his or her two choices for each item.

p. 33
1. undersea
2. zenith
3. enchilada
4. candid
5. section
6. egregious

p. 34
1. L, a
2. DS, c
3. S, b
4. F, d
5. D, c
6. C, d
7. A, d
8. W, c

p. 35
1. crying her eyes out; *meaning:* crying very hard
2. a fish out of water; *meaning:* someone is out of his or her element or in a situation with which he or she is unfamiliar
3. my hands are tied; *meaning:* I can't do anything about this.
4. get cold feet; *meaning:* to back out of something
5. push the envelope; *meaning:* to break the rules or push the limits
6. no dice; *meaning:* I'm not going to do this. OR, I don't agree.

p. 36
1. d
2. d
3. a
4. a, c, and d
5. c and d
6. a
7. e

p. 37
105—Hugh Morrus, comedian
106—Bill D. Bridges engineer
107—Ben Jerelbo, physical therapist
108—Cy Lance, librarian
109—Eaton Wright, nutritionist
115—Ken U. Seamy, optician
116—Chris P. Bacon, chef
117—Sue Yiu, attorney
118—Justin Credabul, magician
119—Caldwell A. Head – reservationist

Other answers will vary. Professions for Buck Kineer and Leigh Vatipp might be pirate and waitress.

p. 38
Answers will vary. Give credit for any explanation that gets at the heart of the pun and adequately explains the word play.

1. *Filet* sounds like *lay*; *filet* is a fishing term, comically replacing another term.
2. Mosquitoes *dive* into skin. The analogy is a clever connection to the sport.
3. The word-play mixes two meanings of the word *armed*.
4. The wordplay mixes two meanings of the word *pool*.
5. The wordplay mixes two meanings of the word *line*.
6. *Shark* replaces *Hark* in a well-known song title.
7. The wordplay mixes two meanings of the word *charging*.
8. The statements themselves are indecisive . . . playing on the word *indecisive*.
9. The wordplay mixes two meanings of the word *combed*, and plays on the homonym for *hair*.
10. The wordplay substitutes the word *red* for its homonym *read* and connects the idea of spending a long time in the sun to the idea of turning red.

Make your vocabulary instruction come alive with interactive whiteboard lessons that teach important skills and capture your students' attention. Contact Incentive Publications for information about the three other Interactive Whiteboard products in this Vocabulary Series:

www.IPinteractive.com

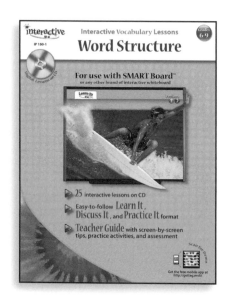

Word Structure

Word Meaning

Confusing Words